When our planet formed about 4500 million years ago, it was very hot, with no atmosphere. Slowly it cooled, and gases collected around the surface. Very simple forms of life developed in shallow pools. They gave off oxygen. The atmosphere gradually changed, and an ozone layer started to form. More complicated kinds of life were able to develop. The atmosphere continued changing, until it reached the mixture it has today. Fish, reptiles and mammals appeared, and finally, humans.

During the last hundred years increasing numbers of humans have been doing things that affect the atmosphere. Oil, coal and gas are being burnt in vast quantities. Cars and aeroplanes pour exhaust fumes into the air. Factories and power stations send their waste products into the air. New products are developed pumping chemicals up into the air. Nuclear explosions and accidents push radioactive pollutants high into the sky. Rockets and satellites litter the upper atmosphere. We make huge amounts of rubbish, much of which is burned. And there are hugely increasing numbers of humans on Earth, and fewer and fewer trees.

Scientists are only now finding out how complex the atmosphere is, and how Earth, water, air and all living things connect, and depend on each other.

We have taken our air for granted. We can't, any more. Understanding what the air is, and how it works, is to learn about our most precious resource. It is part of being able to live successfully on this planet, the Earth, our home.

Photographs: Associated Press 25B
austin j brown 15R, 22T
British Aerospace endpapers, 30, 32–33
Bruce Coleman 12L, 16T, 19BL, 27T
Bruce Coleman/NASA 29R
Colorsport 10T
Daily Telegraph 13B
Image Bank 8, 8–9, 12R, 15L, 16–17, 19T
Jerry Young 16B
Mary Evans Picture Library 14
Meterological Office 19BR, 27B
Military Archive 24
NASA title page, 25T, 33
NHPA/Stephen Dalton 10B
NHPA/Stephen Krazemann 22B
NHPA/Gerard Lacz 11B
Quadrant 23
Royal Aeronautical Society 21TR
Royal Geographical Society 21TL
Science Photo Library/Doug Allan 31
Science Photo Library/Phil Jude cover
Science Photo Library/NASA 28, 29L
Science Photo Library/David Scharf 26, 34
TRH Pictures 11T
ZEFA 17, 21B

Scientific advisor: *Richard Wayne*
Reader in Chemistry
Christ Church
University of Oxford

Design and artwork: *Julia Osorno*

First published in Great Britain in 1990
by Simon & Schuster Young Books

Simon & Schuster Young Books
Simon & Schuster Ltd
Wolsey House, Wolsey Road
Hemel Hempstead, Herts HP2 4SS

British Library Cataloguing in Publication Data
Hooper, Meredith
How high is the sky?
1. Earth's atmosphere
I. Title
523

ISBN 0 7500 0005 8

Contents

Take a breath

Take a breath. Twenty-five million things have just gone inside you. Bits of meteors. Some ash, and sea-salt. Pieces of soil and rock. Moulds and rusts, pollen and fungi. Five or six bacteria. A couple of viruses. Flakes of skin. Droplets of water. Invisible, microscopic things, living and dead, fragments of our planet and rubbish from Space. Unbelievable amounts, all whizzing and tumbling around in the mixture of gases which make up our air.

We live at the bottom of an ocean of air. Air wraps our planet in a warm, soft, moist, blue-coloured layer. We can't hold it, or see it. We take it for granted. But our air is vital to us, and to all living things on Earth.

Earth's atmosphere protects us from the terrible power of the sun. Without our layer of air we would freeze at night in fearful cold, and frizzle in unbearable heat during the day. We would be bombarded by deadly radiation, and pulverized by meteors. Earth's atmosphere is a shield, a filter, a blanket. It is exactly what we need to survive. None of the other planets in our solar system have an atmosphere made of the same mixture of gases. Our atmosphere is unique to Earth.

Take another breath. Each of us breathes ten million times a year. The moment of our birth is the moment of our discovery of air. The moment of our death is when we no longer use it.

What is air? How far up does it go? How high is our sky?

Lift off

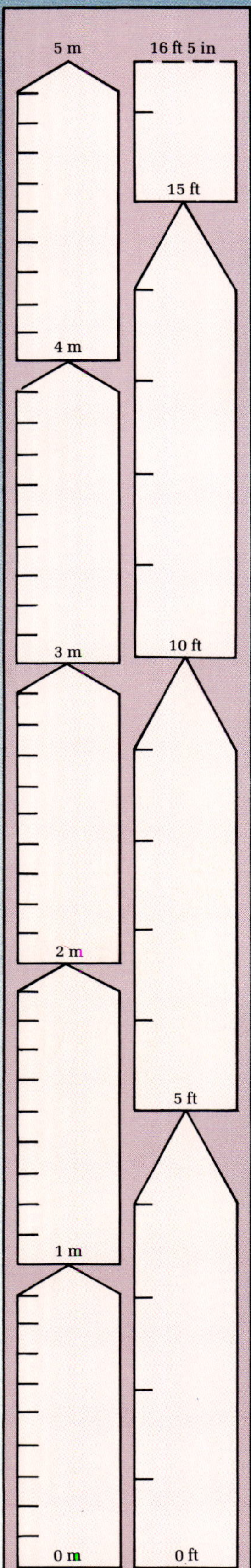

Imagine driving at the motorway speed limit straight up into the sky. You have to drive *straight* up, and keep going at the same speed. Fast. One hundred and twenty kilometres an hour. That's two kilometres every minute. Thirty-three metres a second.

The highest a woman has jumped is 2.09 m (6 ft 10¼ in).

A flea can jump 20 cm (8 in). 130 times its own height

The first successful, controlled, powered aircraft flight rose 3.6 m (12 ft) off the ground and lasted 12 seconds. Orville Wright in South Carolina, USA, 17 December 1903.

The highest jump by a kangaroo is 3.2 m (10 ft 6 in).

Travelling at the motorway speed limit you would take more than four days and nights to drive straight through the centre of the Earth from one side to the other. That's 12,680 kilometres in 106 hours.

Time of journey	**15 seconds**
Distance travelled	**500 metres**
Distance from Earth	**500 metres**

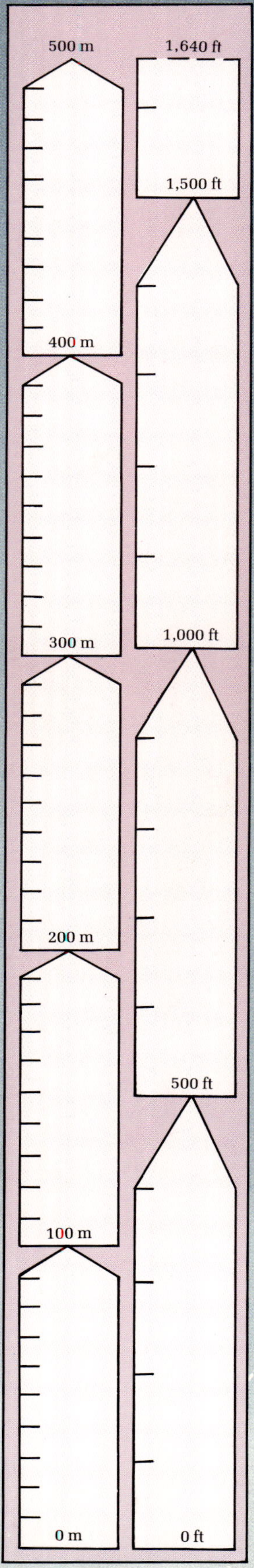

Raindrops fall 1 km (3,300 ft) in 2-4 minutes.

Tallest living thing, Redwood, California, 111.6 m (366 ft 2 in).

Sears Tower, Chicago, built 1973, tallest office building in the world, 110 stories, with television antennae 475,18 m (1,559 ft).

Fog is a cloud on the ground.

A modern airship takes passengers sightseeing at 450 m (1,500 ft).

The Great Pyramid of Cheops, Egypt, built 2580 BC, 146.5 m (480 ft 10 in), the world's tallest building for 4,000 years.

Hold out your hand. You are balancing a column of air, stretching from your skin up into Space. A tonne of air presses down on your head. A kilogram on each finger-nail.

But we don't stagger around under this tremendous weight. Our bodies, and all other things that live on Earth, are adjusted to the pressure of the air. Put us in Space, with no air, and our blood would boil, and our skin explode.

The air next to Earth's surface carries the weight of all the air above, like the bottom blanket in a pile of blankets. A box of air at sea-level, the size of your finger tip, contains 27 million million million (27,000,000,000,000,000,000) particles or molecules of gas. Here, at Earth's surface, the particles of gas are squeezed close together, because of the pressure from the air above. Higher up, with less air pressing down, the particles of gas can spread out. The higher you go the 'thinner' air gets. Fewer particles of gas occupy more and more space.

Our air is a mixture of many gases. Most of air is nitrogen. Oxygen is one fifth. Tiny traces of other gases make up less than one per cent.

The higher we go in the air the less oxygen there is. At five kilometres a lungful of air contains half as much oxygen as at sea level. There is one fifth the amount of oxygen at ten and a half kilometres, where passenger jets cruise. Aircraft carry emergency oxygen in case the cabin air conditioning system fails.

Carbon dioxide is only a very tiny part of our atmosphere. But as we burn more coal and oil, gas and wood, the carbon dioxide increases, helping the air nearest Earth's surface to get warmer. This is the 'greenhouse effect' and it is changing our planet's climate.

Time of journey	**15 seconds**
Distance travelled	**500 metres**
Distance from Earth	**1 kilometre**

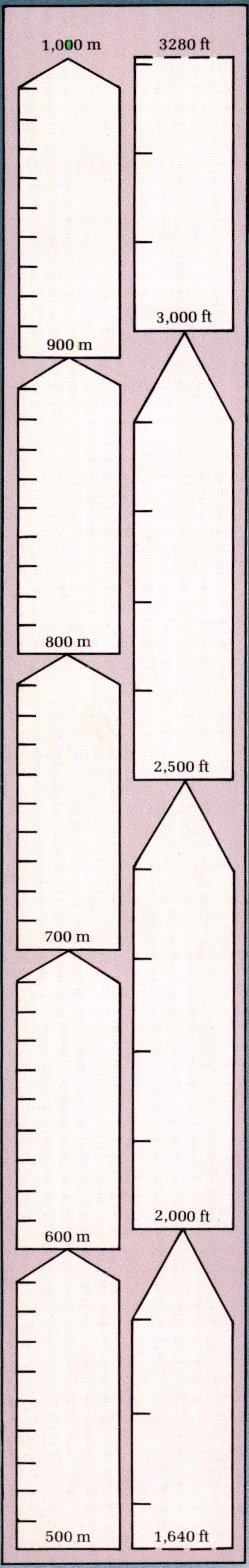

The first parachute jump from a balloon, Paris 22 October 1797, Andre-Jacques Garnerin, at 680 m (2,230 ft).

Every year hundreds of millions of birds leave their summer nesting sites and fly to warm countries where they spend the winter. Migrating birds travel along the same routes, at the same altitudes.

A rainbow's position in the sky can never be measured. Each of us sees our own personal rainbow according to where we are looking from. A rainbow is formed when sunlight strikes drops of water falling from a rain cloud. A rainbow's shape is always part of a circle. The complete circle can never be seen from the ground, but sometimes from an aeroplane.

A balloon can only go where the wind takes it and usually can't return to its launch site. Today, ballooning is a popular sport. Two minutes after launch a modern balloon can be at 900 m (2,952 ft).

Helicopters can fly sideways, backwards, forwards, and hover just off the ground. But over British cities they are not allowed to fly below 450 m (1,500 ft) unless they are being used by the police.

Look up. You might see a bird, or a fly. Start thinking in millions. The air above your head is seething with life. It is home to huge numbers of living things.

All summer millions of insects hang and drift in the air above every square kilometre of England. Birds ride the sky in unbelievable numbers. At the end of summer 5000 million birds leave Europe, and Asia, and fly south to the warmth of Africa.

The insects and birds share the sky with a teeming soup of living things, too small to see.

Most stay close to Earth. There are thirty million microscopic organisms – bacteria, viruses, fungi, yeasts, moulds, algae – in a column of air one kilometre high above your body.

The air carries enough pollen to cover every square metre of the Earth's surface every year with 100 million grains.

People have only recently discovered the size and numbers of this amazing sky zoo. Insects and birds and micro-organisms have been living successfully in the air far longer than humans have been living on Earth.

Time of journey	**1 minute 30 seconds**
Distance travelled	**3 kilometres**
Distance from Earth	**4 kilometres**

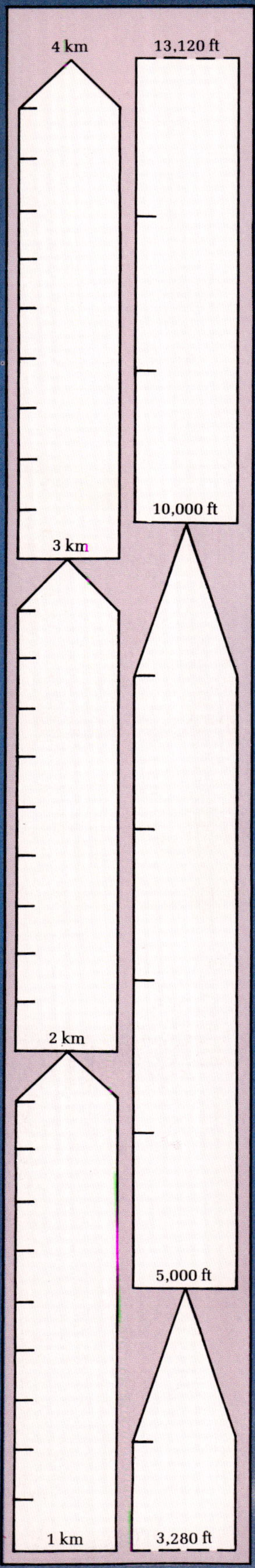

Hawks and eagles use thermals to climb up the sky. They glide slowly down, searching for prey on the ground.

Gliders spiral upwards using rising currents of air called thermals. Glider pilots say thermals are "petrol stations in the sky." "But they are not always where you want them to be."

Stratus is low, grey, level cloud.

The sky isn't really blue. It's black. But radiation from the sun travelling down through the atmosphere strikes molecules of gas, and is scattered by them, making our sky seem bright and blue coloured. If there are a lot of dust particles in the air the scattering produces less blue light, and the sky looks pale, or yellowish. The bluer the sky, the purer the air. Mountains in the distance look blue because of the amount of scattered light between them, and us.

At 3,764 m (12,349 ft) Mt Cook is the highest mountain in New Zealand. It is called 'Cloud Piercer' by the Maoris.

Highest city in the world, Lhasa, Tibet, 3,684 m (12,087 ft).

The air we are breathing now might have been seven kilometres up an hour ago, or twenty kilometres to the west. Our air constantly moves, rising, sinking, mixing, blowing.

Floating and drifting in the air are microscopic bits and pieces from Earth, and Space. There is salt from the ocean. Dust and ash from forest fires, erupting volcanoes, and factory chimneys. Chemicals from power stations, and car and aircraft exhausts. Soil, and clay, and minerals whirled up from Earth's surface. Bits of asbestos, rubber, and paint. Fragments of meteors, and cosmic dust. Most types of particles have always been in the sky. Some are put there by humans.

The heaviest particles fall quickly back to Earth. The smallest drift and blow in the air for days, or weeks. Many are washed out by rain. Some chemicals are washed down as 'acid rain', poisoning lakes, trees and soil.

Time of journey	**1 minute 30 seconds**
Distance travelled	**3 kilometres**
Distance from Earth	**7 kilometres**

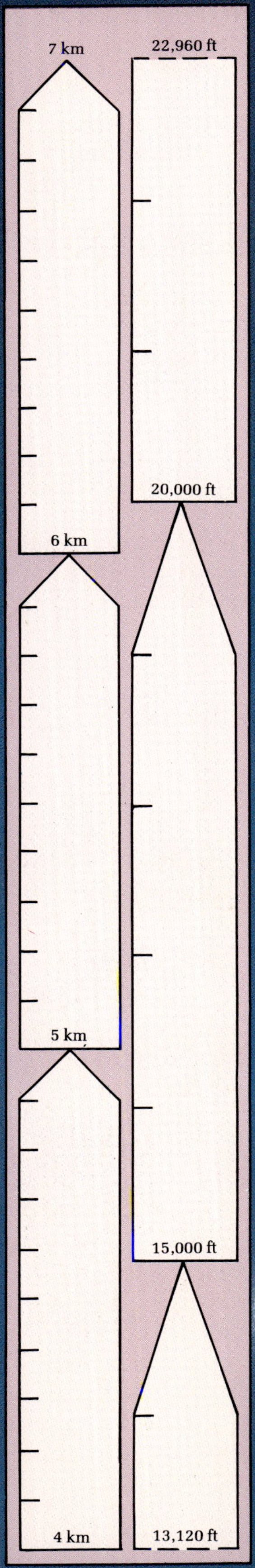

Half the world is always covered by cloud. Clouds help keep the temperature of the Earth neither too hot, nor too cold. They protect us from the sun's heat, and trap warmth rising from the land and the sea. But only five per cent of clouds turn into rain, hail or snow. Most drift away, disappear, or form again somewhere else.

Clouds are collections of ice crystals, or tiny transparent drops of water so small that 50 billion of them wouldn't fill a teacup.

Snow flakes are ice crystals held together with so much air they float lightly, dropping only one to two metres a second. If the air is cold enough they reach the ground as snow. Raindrops are half a millimetre to five millimetres across, and fall two to nine metres a second.

Hailstones are frozen raindrops with violent histories. Caught in powerful seething air currents inside a storm cloud, raindrops can be dragged up into the intense cold of high altitudes, grow a layer of ice, begin falling, be hurled upwards again, until finally, too heavy to be held in the air, they hurtle at high speed out of the cloud to the ground.

Lightning is electricity ripping through the atmosphere, heating a narrow channel of air one centimetre wide, to 10,000 degrees Celsius. In the intense heat the air expands suddenly, then cools, and contracts, causing a sharp crack or echoing rumble of sound. Since sound travels much slower than light, we see the lightning before we hear the thunder.

Lightning flashes nearly nine million times every day. Over mountains a flash might be only 90 m long (300 ft). Over flat land the flash may reach down 6 km (4 miles) to Earth.

There is half as much oxygen at 5,600 m (18,000 ft) as at sea-level. Winds blow fiercely. The air is thin and there is little to slow them down.

Billowy heaped-up clouds with sharp edges called cumulus are made of water droplets and some ice crystals. Powerful air currents can be rushing up and down inside their soft-looking bodies.

Highest mountain in USA, Mt McKinley, 6,193 m (20,320 ft).

Thousands of meteorological balloons filled with hydrogen are released every day. They carry instruments to measure the temperature, pressure and moisture of the air.

Butterflies can be lifted to 6100 m (20,000 ft) and swept huge distances across the sea by strong winds. Many species of butterfly are tough long-distance migrants travelling up to 100 km (60 miles) a day. They follow set routes and navigate by the sun.

Time of journey	**1 minute 30 seconds**
Distance travelled	**3 kilometres**
Distance from Earth	**10 kilometres**

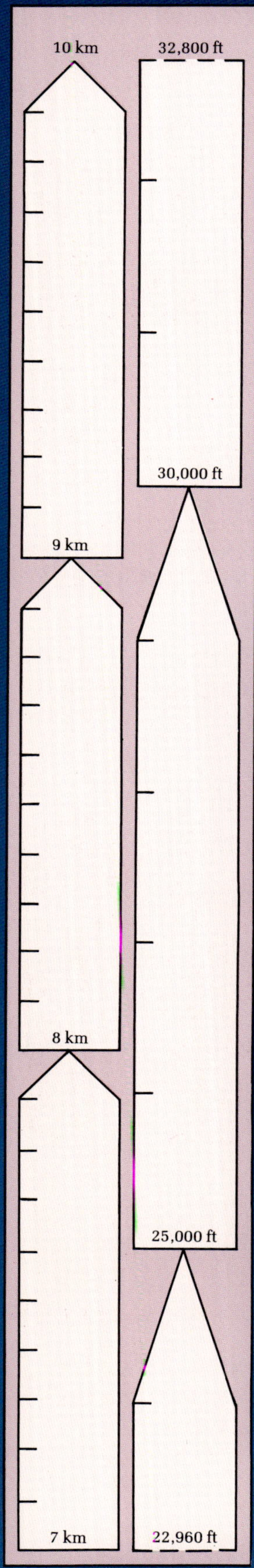

The sky is in layers, like wrapping paper. In the layer nearest the Earth all our weather happens, good and bad. Here the air is forever moving. Insects, animals and microscopic creatures float and fly. Here are clouds, and water vapour, and dust.

The temperature drops with height, steadily, but not always evenly. On average the temperature drops one degree Celsius every 150 metres. About 11 kilometres above Earth the temperature stops falling, and sticks at around minus 60 degrees.

The lid on the layer nearest the Earth is made of this very cold air. The lid shifts up and down, depending on the time of year, and the time of day. But it is always lowest over the poles, and highest over the equator.

A child's balloon filled with hydrogen reaches about 9 km (30,000 ft) before bursting.

If the air is cold enough the exhausts from jet engines make long thin artificial clouds called vapour trails.

The temperature can be −40°C, −40°F, at 10 km (32,000 ft)

Rivers of air howl around the Earth 9 to 12 km (30–40,000 ft) up, as fast as 400 kph (250 mph). Aircraft can catch these jet streams and arrive faster than usual. Flying the other way against the jet stream takes longer than usual.

High whispy white clouds called cirrus are made of ice crystals, swirling and cascading through the thin air. They look as if they are moving slowly. But they can travel at 160 kph (100 mph).

The latest satellite measurements put Mt Everest, the world's highest mountain, at 8,863 m (29,078 ft). At the top the air presses down with less than a third the weight of air at sea level. Everest was first climbed in 1953 by Sir Edmund Hillary and Sherpa Tensing.

There are 109 mountains above 7,315 m (24,000 ft).

The first aeroplane to fly higher than the highest point on Earth, Mt Everest, was a Nieuport Biplane, 26 May 1919. It reached 29,937 ft.

Passenger aircraft fly through the sky obeying strict traffic rules. They fly along special routes, like corridors, which are marked on maps. The sky is divided into layers for safer flying. The layers, called flight levels, are measured in feet the world-over. Below 29,000 ft each layer is 1,000 ft deep, above, each layer is 2,000 ft deep.

Four fifths of all the Earth's atmosphere is in the first layer. It is called the troposphere, and the lid is known as the tropopause.

We have taken five minutes to drive through it, at motorway speed.

Time of journey	**10 minutes**
Distance travelled	**20 kilometres**
Distance from Earth	**30 kilometres**

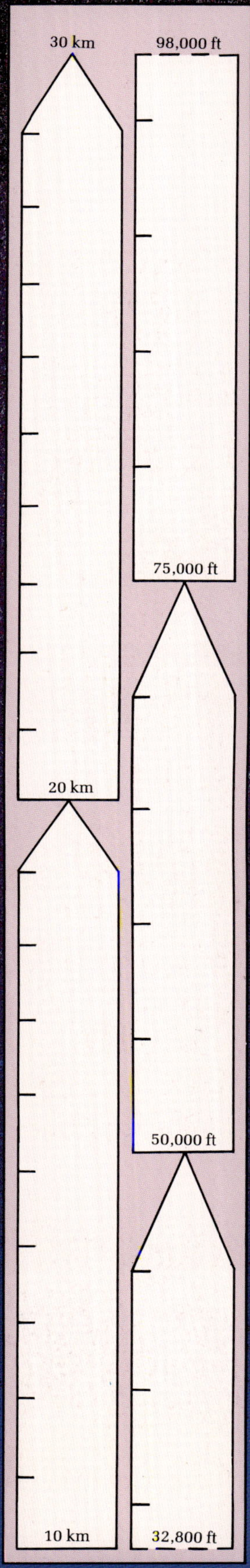

Painted black to reduce its temperature the Lockheed Blackbird SR-71A reconnaissance plane holds the world speed and sustained height record: 2,983 mph at 78,750 ft. Flying at Mach 3 the Blackbird carries infra-red cameras able to photograph a strip of the Earth's surface 200 km (120 miles) wide.

A greater snow goose flying 70 mph at 33,000 ft hit the nose of a 747 jet over Newfoundland in November 1988.

The second layer of sky, the stratosphere, is clear and peaceful. There is very little mixing between the heaving air of the bottom layer, and the quiet air up here. The air is very thin. A human would become unconscious in seconds from lack of oxygen.

Every now and then something from Earth punches up through the bottom layer of air and brings pollutants into the stratosphere. Erupting volcanoes and nuclear explosions have shot dust and debris 50 kilometres high.

Once in the stratosphere, particles of dust and chemicals can stay for years. Spread sideways by winds they form a layer dimming the power of the sun.

The stars shine all day at 21 kilometres. Here the sky is a violet-grey colour, shading to greyish-black. Three kilometres higher the sun shines out of a perfectly black sky. There aren't enough molecules of gas to scatter the light.

Ozone is spread very very thinly in a layer from about 15 km (9 miles) to 40 km (25 miles) above Earth.

Concorde cruises at Mach 2, at 50,000-60,000 ft.

Time of journey	**10 minutes**
Distance travelled	**20 kilometres**
Distance from Earth	**50 kilometres**

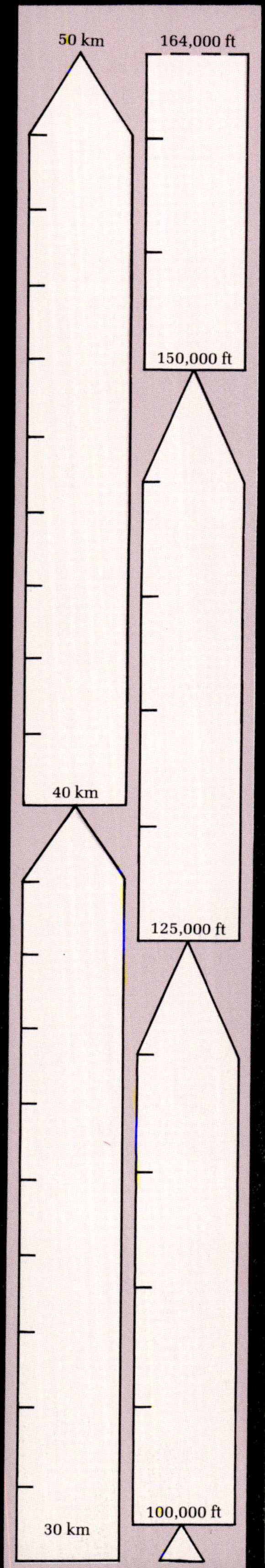

The sun pours out a huge amount of heat. Our Earth collects only a tiny part. Eight minutes and twenty seconds after leaving the sun, waves of heat meet the outer edges of our atmosphere, and travel, in one thousandth of a second, to Earth's surface.

During the journey through our atmosphere some of the sun's radiation is turned back into Space. Some is absorbed by molecules of gas. Some gets through to Earth's surface, heating the land and the oceans.

People can see part of the sun's radiation. We see it as light, in the colours which appear in a rainbow – red, orange, yellow, green, blue, indigo and violet. Beyond the red light is infra-red which we can't see, but some animals can. Beyond the violet light are ultra-violet, and X-rays, which we also cannot see.

Ultra-violet is dangerous to humans, and most living things. In the stratosphere ultra-violet radiation crashes and zaps into molecules of oxygen. Some of the oxygen molecules split apart. They form a gas called ozone. This absorbs ultra-violet radiation. The ozone is spread very very thinly through a 25 kilometre layer of sky.

The world altitude record in an aircraft, 123,524 ft was reached on 31 August 1977 by Aleksandr Fedotov in a MiG-25.

Ozone is a smelly poisonous gas. Down on Earth it can form in cities as a pollutant. But up here in the stratosphere, it is an invisible shield, a protecting screen for life on Earth. We depend on it for our survival.

Chemicals, which destroy ozone, are slowly but surely working their way up into the stratosphere. Chemicals used in refrigerators, foam packaging, air-conditioning and aerosols can release atoms of the element chlorine in the stratosphere. Each atom of chlorine can destroy hundreds of thousands of molecules of ozone. Every year a large hole develops in the ozone layer over the Antarctic.

The ozone layer began 3,000 million years ago. Humans started making the products which attack ozone 60 years ago. But we only found out about the damage recently.

The Space Shuttle's booster rockets separate from the fuel tank 2 minutes 3 seconds after take-off, at 44,200 m (27.6 miles). They fall into the sea five and half minutes later.

Captain Joseph Kittinger made the world's longest parachute drop when he stepped from the gondola of a helium-filled balloon on 16 August 1960 at 31,333 m (102,800 ft). He fell 26 km (16 miles) before opening his parachute, reaching a speed of 1130 kph (702 mph).

Time of journey	**20 minutes**
Distance travelled	**40 kilometres**
Distance from Earth	**90 kilometres**

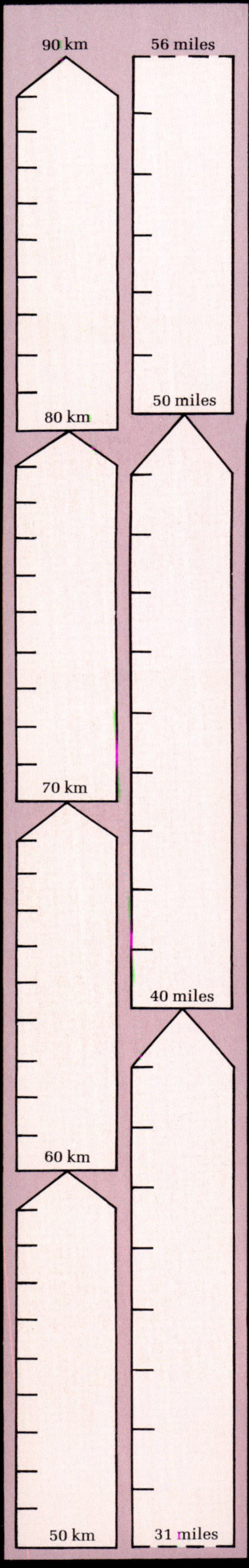

The stratosphere is cold at the bottom, where Concorde flies, and warms up in the ozone layer. The ozone layer's hot upper edge is the boundary of the stratosphere, the stratopause. There is so little oxygen here a candle couldn't burn.

Thirty kilometres higher is the coldest place in the sky, minus 143 degrees Celsius. This layer, where the temperature falls rapidly, is called the mesosphere. It ends in the mesopause.

Almost all Earth's atmosphere is in the first 80 kilometres of sky. Here the air is made up of the same general mixture of gases. Above, the amounts and types of gases change. But there is still enough to stop meteors, and slow down Space ships, to bounce radio waves, and fundamentally affect what happens on Earth.

Russian rockets collected bacteria and fungi at heights between 58 km and 75 km (36 miles and 46 miles), in 1974. These included the fungus Aspergillus niger *which causes inflammation of the ear.*

Every day the Earth collides with hundreds of millions of tiny meteors. Speeding into the atmosphere between 80 km and 120 km (50 miles and 75 miles), they burn up in one or two seconds.

Mesosphere means middle sphere or layer. At the top of the mesosphere is a 10 km layer where the temperature is extremely cold, the mesopause.

The highest clouds of all, rare and mysterious, float near the mesopause, five times higher than most other clouds. These noctilucent clouds are made of ice crystals, or tiny grains of Space dust, each particle coated with ice.

Time of journey	**3 hours 25 minutes**
Distance travelled	**410 kilometres**
Distance from Earth	**500 kilometres**

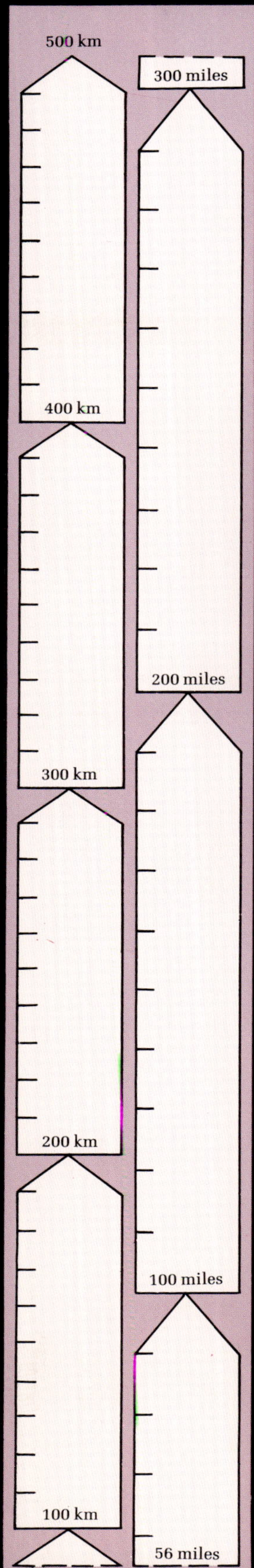

The atmosphere gets very hot, very fast, above 90 kilometres. The temperature changes wildly between day and night. Ultra-violet, infra-red, X-rays, pour in from the sun. Cosmic rays pour in from Space. This is Earth's first line of defence. It is called the thermosphere, which means hot layer.

Radio signals sent up from Earth are bounced back by particles of gas which act like reflecting mesh.

The bus-sized Hubble Space Telescope was launched on 24 April 1990 on board the Space Shuttle Discovery. It orbits at 608 km (380 miles) above Earth's murky atmosphere, photographing objects in the Universe.

A view of a hurricane from 200 km (125 miles) above Earth. Hurricane Elena photographed on 2 September 1985 from the Space Shuttle Discovery.

Violent activity in the sun can heat up the atmosphere, puffing it out in a bulge. When this happens spy satellites orbiting 200 kilometres above Earth are slowed because they have to pass through more gas particles. Their useful life is shortened.

Meteors hurtle towards Earth. Bits of rock, or iron, they streak in at 30 kilometres a second. Somewhere between 120 and 80 kilometres away from Earth's surface they crash into molecules of gas, and burn.

'Shooting stars' are meteors big enough to leave a brief bright trail of gas, dust and ash as they vaporize. They range in size from a grain of sand to a raisin. Each day as many as 10 meteors may be heavy enough to break through the atmosphere and reach Earth's surface as meteorites. But every day billions more, less than one millimetre across, are pulverised in the upper atmosphere.

The Space Shuttle's empty fuel tank is jettisoned just before the Shuttle goes into orbit and 10 seconds after the main engines stop burning. The tank is 47 m (154 ft) long and breaks up in the atmosphere, scattering into the Indian Ocean.

The Shuttle orbits at 200 km (125 miles).

Challenger in orbit, Photographed by Bruce McCandless on 7 February 1984; the first human to walk unattached in Space.

Time of journey	**12 hours 30 minutes**
Distance travelled	**1,500 kilometres**
Distance from Earth	**2,000 kilometres**

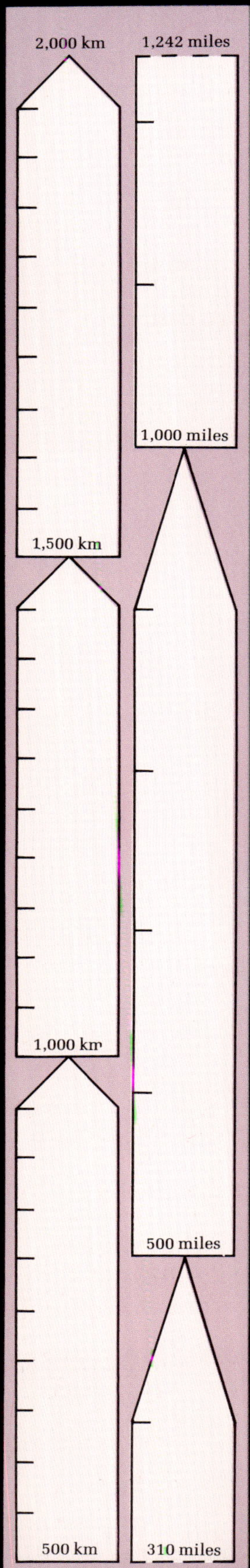

The atmosphere is extremely thin around 500 kilometres from Earth. Particles of air are so far apart they hardly ever collide. With so few collisions to slow them down particles soar, and orbit, travelling on and up. The force of Earth's gravity pulls most back down. But some, moving at 40,000 kilometres per hour, escape.

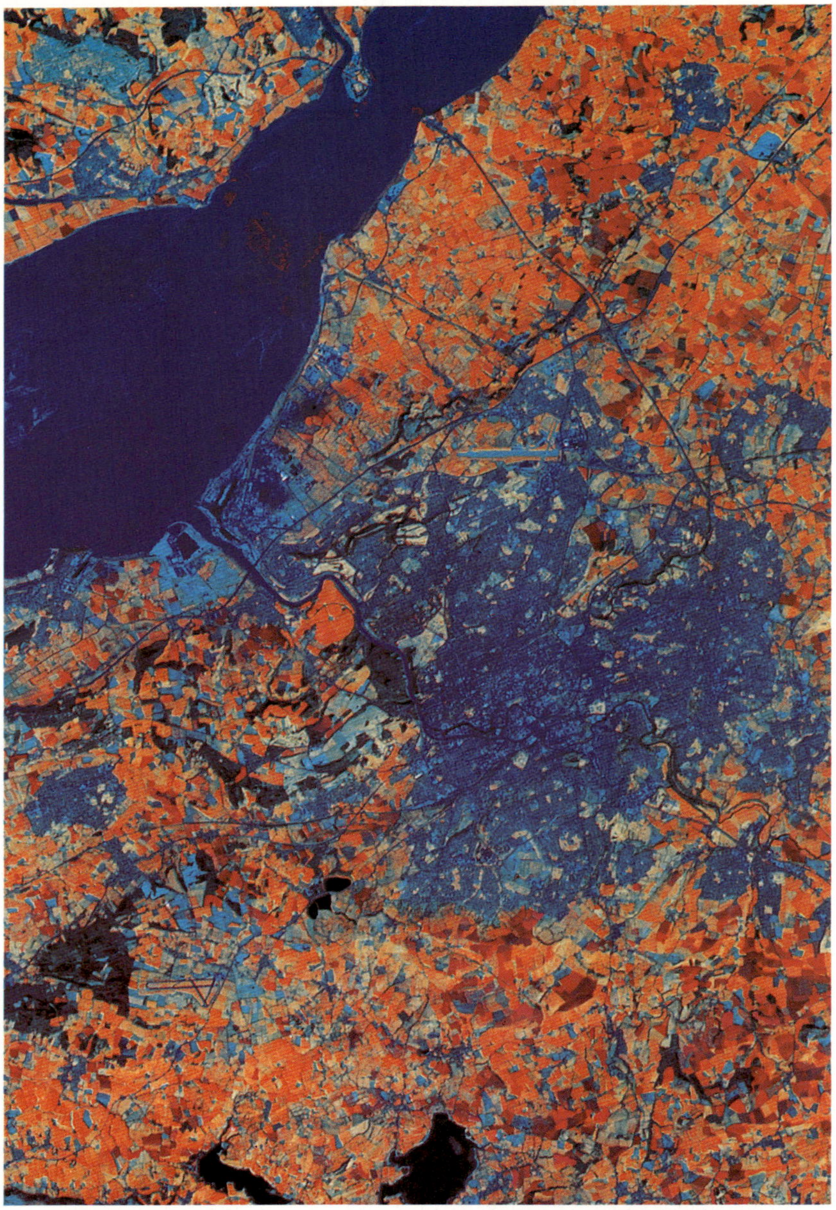

The Bristol area, UK, in April 1984 seen from the American Landsat 5 satellite orbiting at 705 km (440 miles). The picture was taken in the infra-red part of the spectrum. People cannot see infra-red and the colours were added by computer to give an image they could see. The colours mean the following;

dark greyish brown – deciduous woodland
dark reddish brown – coniferous woodland
pale olive – rough grassland
orange – managed grassland
strong red/reddish brown – green crops
blue – bare soil
dark blue – water
strong blue – urban areas
blue/ brown speckle – houses

This outermost part of the atmosphere, where escapes happen, is called the exosphere. The air is mostly made up of the lightest gases of all, helium and hydrogen.

Most satellites orbit here: weather satellites, navigation and spy satellites, satellites which survey crops, or search for oil.

But only about five per cent of objects in orbit are actually working. Many have exploded, or broken down. Since the world's first satellite began orbiting on 4 October 1957, there has been one new launch into Space every three days, on average. Over 7,000 separate chunks of satellite or rocket, each piece more than 10 centimetres in size, are now whizzing through the exosphere, between 500 and 2,000 kilometres up. There are too many fragments smaller than 10 centimetres to count.

Satellites orbiting lower, at 200 kilometres, are slowed down by particles of air. Eventually, pulled towards Earth by the force of gravity, they plunge out of orbit, explode, and destroy themselves. But higher up, in the exosphere, each piece of Space junk can last thousands of years. Travelling at 27,000 kilometres an hour, it is dangerous stuff. A tiny speck of paint from an old rocket, just one fifth of a millimetre across, cracked a Space ship window in 1983. This last layer of our atmosphere is being cluttered with our rubbish.

Beautiful curtains of coloured light sometimes hang in long curving shimmering sheets in the northern and southern skies. Red, purple, blue, these auroras glow anywhere between 100 km and 1,000 km (60 miles and 600 miles) up. They are caused by particles from the sun which spiral in towards the magnetic poles and hit molecules of gas.

An aurora Australis photographed in Antarctica.

Time of journey	**11 days 19 hours**
Distance travelled	**34,000 kilometres**
Distance from Earth	**36,000 kilometres**

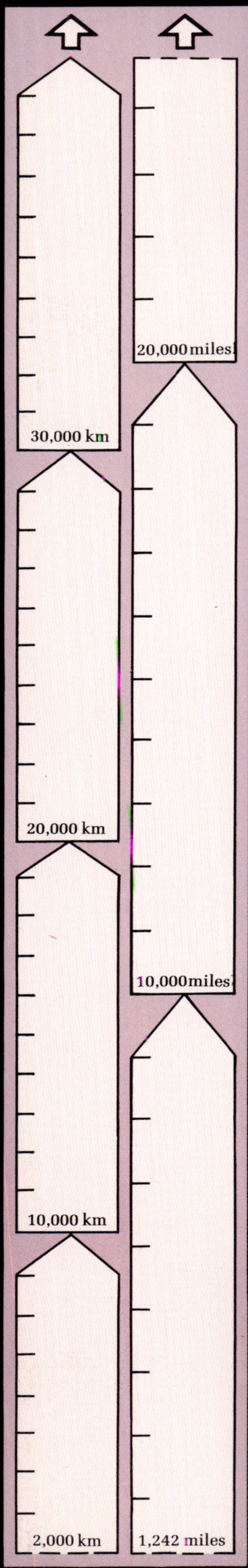

The air is a coat of gases wrapped around the Earth. Most of it lies in a thin layer, like the skin on an apple. We could drive through it, at motorway speed, in five minutes.

After four and a quarter hours driving at the same speed we would reach the part of our sky where the gases of our atmosphere begin to leak away into Space.

Far beyond, a few molecules of air still swing and soar. But Space isn't empty. It is filled with particles streaming from the sun. It seethes with radioactive energy. Earth's atmosphere mixes with the sun's, colliding, interacting.

At 36,000 kilometres above Earth, communications satellites orbit, transmitting television, telephone and computer data. A television signal takes a quarter of a second to travel from the studio to the satellite and back to a television set. But nothing must be in the way, not even the leaves of a tree.

Here at the satellites we are one eleventh of the way to the moon. The moon is 3,200 hours driving at motorway speed from the Earth. One and a quarter million hours driving gets us to the sun. And the nearest star, Proxima Centauri, is 28,000 times further away than the sun.

How high is the sky? We are still finding out.

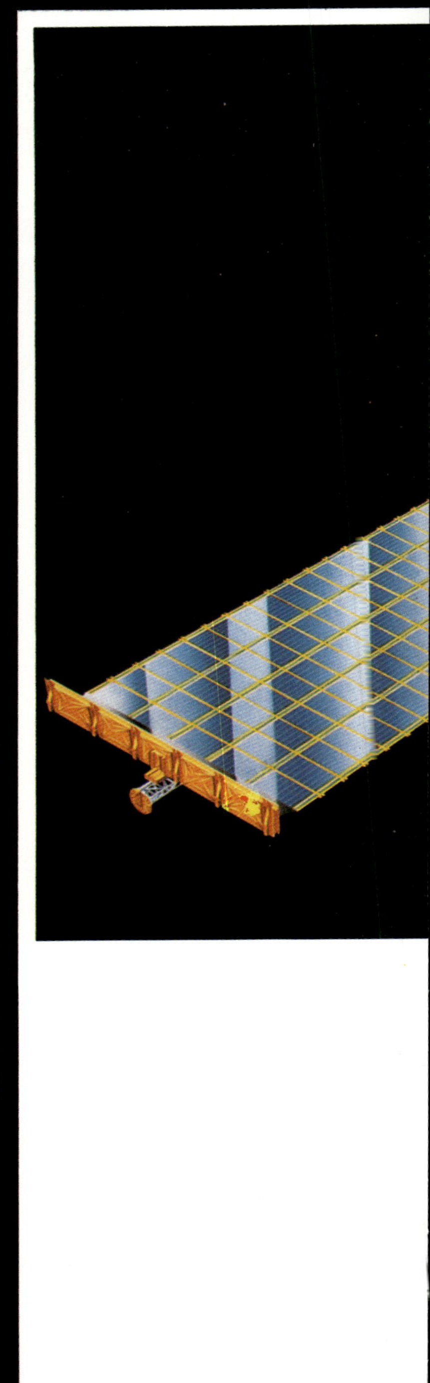

At 35,786 km (22,366 miles) a satellite is the exact height to be above the equator and to keep in time with the Earth as it spins. This allows the satellite to stay above the same place on Earth's surface. It is known as geostationary orbit.

Olympus 1 is a communications satellite launched in July 1989 by the European Space Agency. From its geostationary orbit it handles television, video-conferencing, tele-education, remote printing and data distribution.

At 36,000 km above the equator the American satellite ATS-111 sent back this photograph of our planet showing Europe, Greenland, Africa, part of North and South America and Antarctica.

Further information

Sneeze once, in a room, and up to a million tiny droplets fly out of your nose and mouth, travelling at 400 metres per second. Half the droplets carry bacteria. The droplets and bacteria join with the other particles in the air. But open the window, and they begin moving outside into the sky. There they mix with the 5,600 million million (5,600,000,000,000,000) tonnes of air in our atmosphere.

Describing the atmosphere means thinking very big, and very small.

Air pressure
A quarter of our air is in the 2·5 km nearest Earth. Half is below 5·6 km. Three quarters is below 10·3 km. Only one part in a hundred is above 31.2 km. One part in a thousand is above 48·1 km. Only two parts in a million are above 100 km.

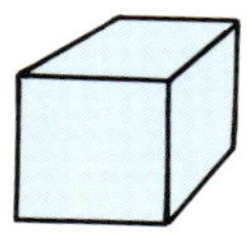

One cubic centimetre of air at sea level contains 27 million million million (27,000,000,000,000,000,000) molecules of gas, each travelling at 1,600 kph, and colliding 5,000 million (5,000,000,000) times a second. Six hundred kilometres up in the sky the molecules of gas are so spaced out they travel 10 km before colliding.

The gases in our air
The mixture of gases that makes up dry air in our atmosphere is the same for the first 80 km:

Nitrogen	Oxygen	Argon
78·08%	20·9%	0·9%

Other gases for example neon, helium, methane, krypton, xenon, hydrogen, ozone, make up only one hundredth of one per cent.

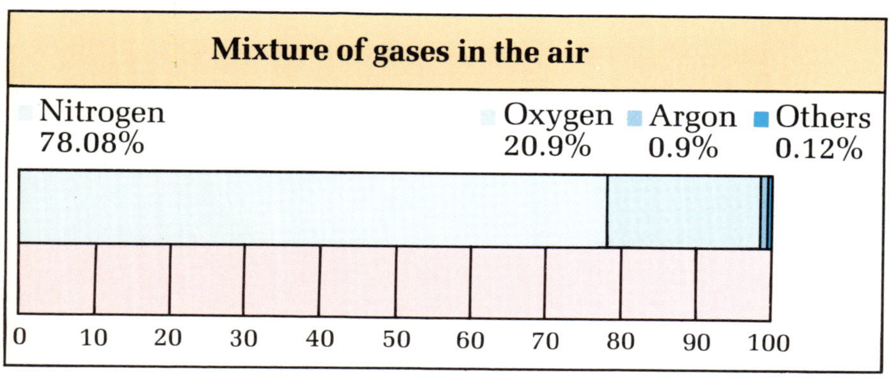

All living things that breathe, take in oxygen from the air and give out carbon dioxide. Plants take in carbon dioxide, and give out oxygen. Carbon dioxide is now 0·035% of the atmosphere, 25% more than in 1850.

Water in the atmosphere
Water is present in the atmosphere as a gas (water vapour), as a liquid (water droplets, mist, rain), and as a solid (crystals of ice or snow). Water vapour varies between 0·01% and 4·0% of the atmosphere.

Water is being constantly sucked up into the air, and falling back again, onto the land and sea. There are 500 million million (500,000,000,000,000) tonnes of water in our atmosphere at any one time. Even then, that is only one thousandth of one per cent of all the water on Earth. If it fell all at once it would cover the entire surface of the planet in 2·5 cm of rain.

Particles in the air
Mixed in with the gases of Earth's atmosphere are minute particles of liquid and solid matter so small they can only be seen with powerful microscopes. Many are less than one thousandth of a millimetre across.

Human skin in household dust

Picture enlarged ×1650

Ten thousand particles float in every cubic centimetre of our air. Above our cities the number of particles can be fifteen times greater.

It is difficult to imagine how small these particles are. Our skin constantly sheds tiny flakes of dead cells. Hundreds of thousands float invisibly above a bed just after it has been made. One skin flake is eight thousandths of a millimetre across, about the same size as a water droplet in a cloud. But it is wide enough to carry a whole colony of bacteria. About 656 million of the smallest known bacteria can fill the space occupied by the head of a pin. A flu virus is six times smaller than the smallest known bacteria. Viruses, bacteria, water, droplets, skin cells, join particles of salt, soot, dust, smoke, chemicals and other substances in the atmosphere. The cleanest air, breathed on board a yacht in the Pacific Ocean, contains about 200,000 of these particles in every lungful (half a litre) of air. In a city rush hour air can be packed with 375 million particles for every half litre breathed.

The sun

A large hot object like the sun gives out a tremendous amount of energy. It gives the light and warmth we need for life here on Earth. But the sun also gives off deadly radiation, and a stream of particles travelling through Space called the 'solar wind'.

Energy from the sun reaches Earth in the form of waves. Different kinds of radiation have different wavelengths. Visible light is made up of seven colours each with its own wavelength. X-rays and gamma rays have shorter wavelengths and microwaves and radio waves have longer ones.

The atmosphere keeps the sun's deadly radiation from Earth's surface. The solar wind is kept away by the huge magnetic envelope of Earth's magnetic field. The solar wind cannot cross this envelope, which loops 64,000 km out towards the sun. The solar wind flows around it, as if the Earth and its magnetic field were a rock in the sea.

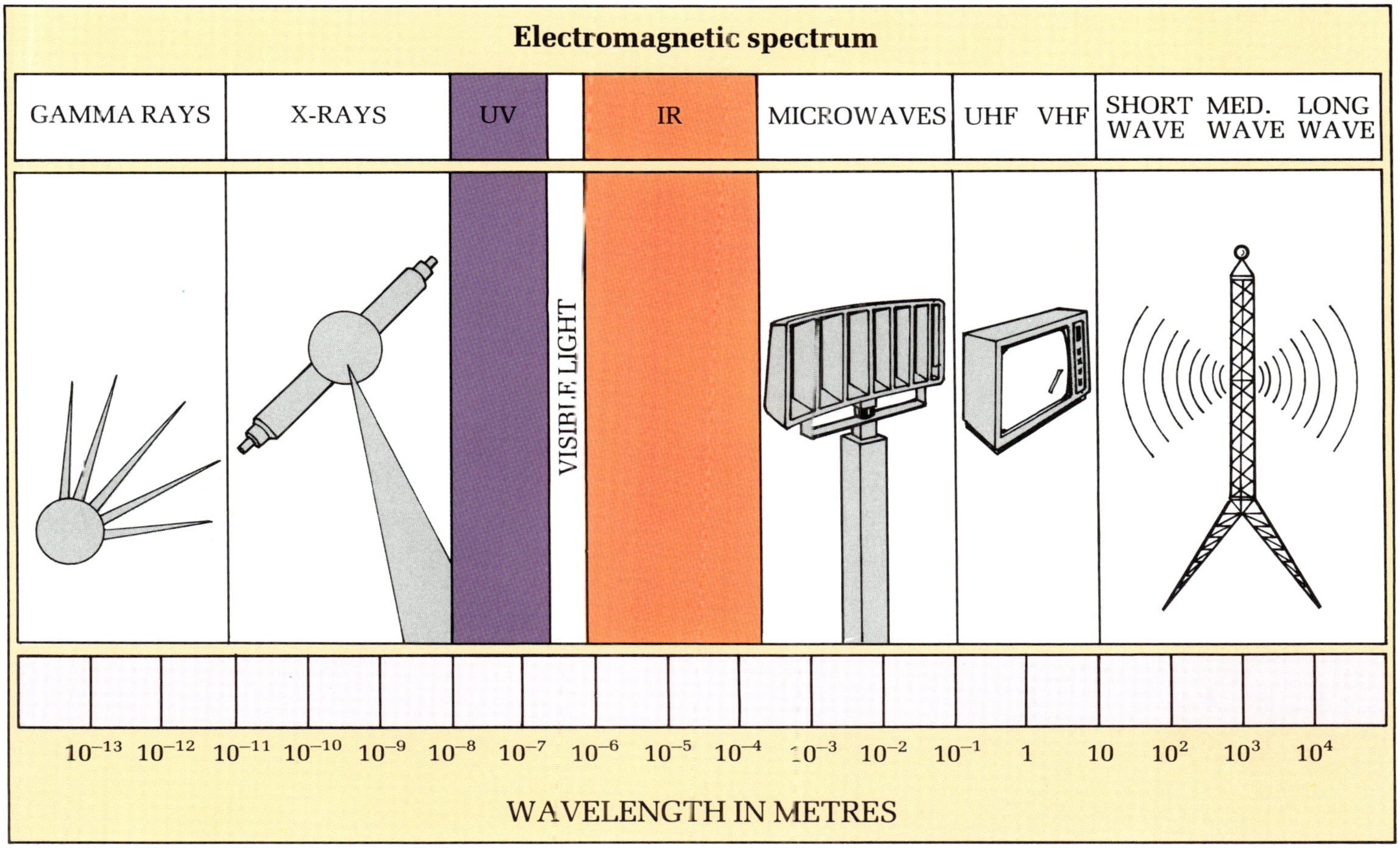

The layers in the atmosphere

Scientists could only begin studying and measuring the air higher than mountains in the 19th century when they rode up into the atmosphere in baskets slung under big balloons. They could only begin studying and measuring the upper atmosphere after the first satellites were launched in the late 1950s.

Scientists discovered that the air is arranged in layers which can be described according to temperature, types of gases, number of particles, or living things, amount of water vapour, the pressure of air. Names have been agreed for the layers, and their heights above the surface of Earth, although heights can vary with time and place.

The lowest layer, the troposphere, rises 8 km over the poles, and 16–17 km over the equator. The temperature drops with height, 1°C for every 150 m climbed. At the top of the troposphere (the tropopause) the temperature sticks at about −60°C.

In the stratosphere ultra-violet rays collide with oxygen, warming the atmosphere. The temperature is highest at the stratopause (about 50 km), where the air can sometimes be as warm as at the surface of Earth.

The temperature drops again in the mesosphere. The lowest temperatures in the atmosphere happen at the mesopause (about 80 km).

The thermosphere is five times deeper than all the other layers below. It merges into the exosphere around 500 km. The temperature increases rapidly.

There are electrically charged particles in the atmosphere, which affect radio waves. Some radio waves are absorbed, and some are bent back down to Earth. These electrically charged particles are concentrated in a region of the atmosphere scientists call the 'ionosphere'. It stretches from about 60 km above Earth to somewhere between 200 km and 400 km.

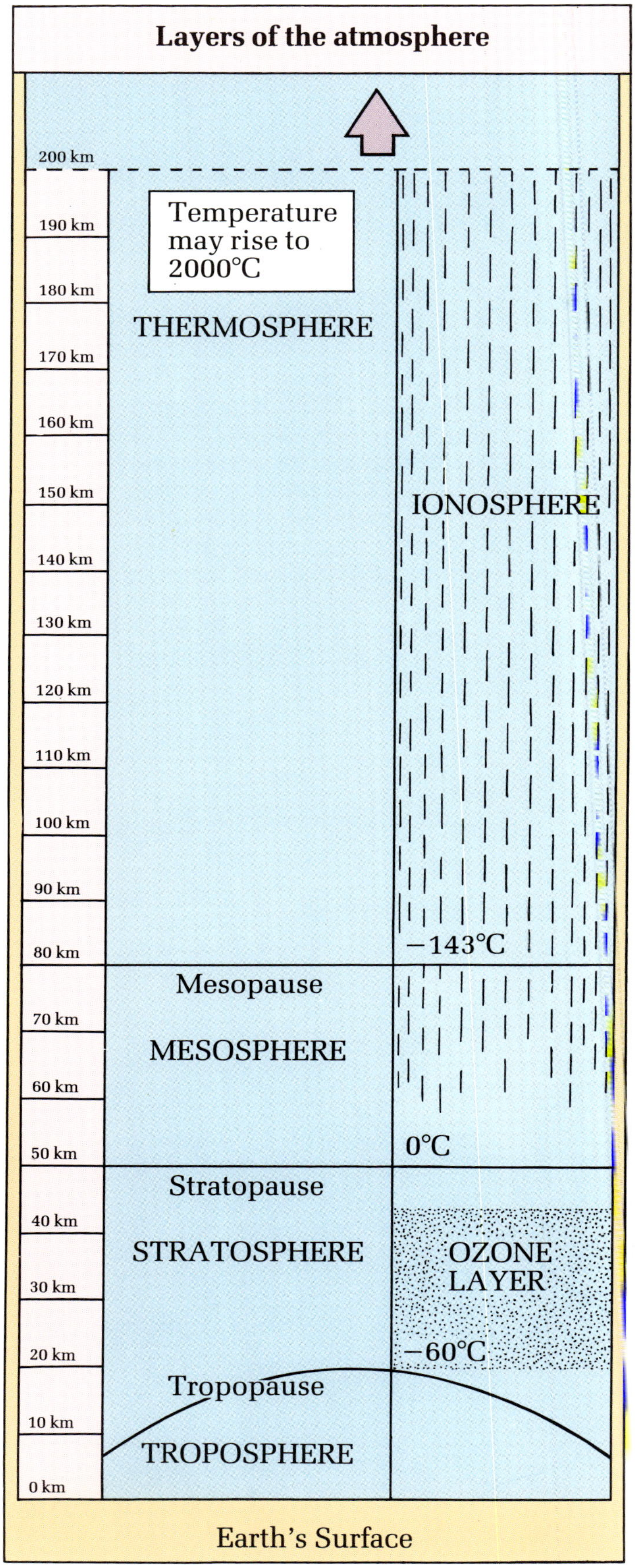

Index

Page numbers in **heavy type** refer to pictures.
Page numbers in *slanted type* refer to information in captions.

Endpaper:
The Gemini/Agena Spacecraft orbits 180–240 km (113–150 miles) above Earth.